Do Not Stop the Little Children

LEAVE THE WAY OPEN FOR MY LITTLE ONES

Mary Marriott

Kingdom Publishers

Do Not Stop the Little Children
Leave the Way Open for My Little Ones
Copyright© Mary Marriott

All rights reserved. No part of this book may be
reproduced in any form by photocopying or any
electronic or mechanical means, including information
storage or retrieval systems, without permission in
writing from both the copyright owner and the publisher
of the book. The right of Mary Marriott to be identified as the author of this
work has been asserted by her in
accordance with the Copyright, Designs and Patents Act
1988 and any subsequent amendments thereto.
A catalogue record for this book is available from the
British Library.
All Scripture Quotations have been taken from the
New King James Version of the Bible.

ISBN: 978-1-911697-31-2

1st Edition by Kingdom Publishers

Kingdom Publishers
London, UK.

You can purchase copies of this book from any leading bookstore or
email **contact@kingdompublishers.co.uk**

DEDICATED TO THE GLORY OF GOD

How could I refuse to write this little book? As a mother of five precious, now adult children, I have, over a period of years, become more and more concerned about children not having a proper childhood. I knew it to be on God's heart, and realised He wanted me to write about it. I thought it would have to be hundreds of pages and I didn't feel up to the writing. However, I soon discerned that it was the message that was important, not the number of words and pages, so I set out to write for ours and God's 'little people'. Parents of these invaluable gifts have a deep responsibility, as it is no easy task bringing up children 'in the way they should go' - but what a privilege.

DO NOT STOP THE LITTLE CHILDREN

TO BE A CHILD

Sweet child,
a star sent down from heaven,
perhaps divine, who knows?
Nine months to grow
within a cave of darkness,
a cave of warmth and comfort,
a hiding place 'til birth takes place.
A scream, a shout
and out she floats
on board the boat of life,
where calm and strife
will follow her along the way
and she will walk in peace,
at times to stray awhile
when no longer child.
But let us see
and know her innocence,

this gift bestowed
upon the likes of us.
The gentleness of hands and feet;
a shriek of glee
when bouncing on a knee,
and in the bath,
we can only laugh
as water splashes in her face
and then the race to dry
before the plughole swallows all;
glug, glug, sigh.
The love, the trust, a glowing from within;
she is bathed in innocence, no sin.

Matthew 18:2-7 Then Jesus called a little child to Him, set him in the midst of them and said, "Assuredly, I say to you, unless you are converted and become as little children, you will by no means enter the kingdom of heaven. Therefore, whoever humbles himself as this little child is the greatest in the kingdom of heaven. Whoever receives one little child like this in My name receives Me; <u>But whoever causes one of these little ones who believes in Me to sin</u>, it would be better for him if a millstone were hung around his neck, and he were

drowned in the depth of the sea; Woe to the world because of offences! For offences must come, but woe to that man by whom the offence comes."** (underlining mine)

And to go on from that we read in **Chapter 19:14-15 Then the little children were brought to Him that He might put His hands on them and pray, but the disciples rebuked them. But Jesus said, "<u>Let the little children come to Me and do not forbid them; for of such is the Kingdom of Heaven</u>," and He laid His hands on them and departed from there.** (underlining mine)

Are we preventing our little ones from knowing their Saviour by our actions that are worldly, distracting them in ways that are not pleasing to God?

This is a very serious and in depth question, and its importance cannot be emphasised enough.

The preciousness of children in God's eyes is immeasurable, and He blessed them to human kind to be cherished.

There are, of course, many parents who do just that – and…....

Train up a child in the way that he should go. And when he is old he will not depart from it. Proverbs 22:6.

And the reason for this strictness is that they are aware of - as we read in **Proverbs 22:15 Foolishness is bound up in the heart of a child; the rod of correction will drive it far from him.**

It is important to keep in mind **Proverbs 23:13** which follows, though it is a difficult one to take on board and mainly because the way it is worded. It may sound cruel, especially in today's society where there are health and safety rules, (which have, by 'going over the top', brought on the lack of discipline and led to so many going astray.) It is a discipline, but of course, must be done in love, therefore one doesn't beat the child to pulp.

Do not withhold correction from a child, for if you beat him with a rod, he will not die. You shall beat him with a rod, and deliver his soul from hell.

To word it differently, but with the same meaning - 'Tell your child off, give him a smack if necessary, for this will not harm him, but firm discipline will hold him in good stead and prevent him from perishing.'

We live in a very unhappy society. Many fool themselves into thinking otherwise, that they are fulfilled and happy. Social media exploits them at a young age, putting them in a mind set from which, if we are not wise, there is no escape.

They are in a spiders web.

A SPIDER AND HIS WEB

Have you ever watched a spider spin his web?
It's an extraordinary phenomenon indeed,
and it doesn't really take much of his time,
for he's pretty smart and quick, in fact he's rather slick.
When you have a minute, maybe three or four, no more,

and spy one, (in the garden is the best) just watch.
The speed and intricacies are plain to see;

a work of art there is no doubt, something you and I could never do; it's quite amazing, fascinating.

When the web's been spun, it's really so much fun to stay and watch the spider's little antics. In the centre of his web he tires his silken thread, steps aside and waits along the edge. Soon an insect falls into the sticky mesh; the spider darts out at quite a speed and wraps up his tasty dish, leaves it there to die, and exits back to keep another watchful eye for an insect or a fly to enter his exquisite silky trap.

If Christian parents are immersed too much in the modern way of life, it leaves little scope for their children not to follow them. No-one is perfect, everyone is human, but even followers of Christ will not enter His glory unless they become perfect – so says Jesus.

Therefore you should be perfect, just as your Father in heaven is perfect. Matthew 5:48.

Does that sound unreasonable? How on earth can we be perfect you might ask. It's impossible. Yes, it is – in our own strength. A lot of things in life are impossible, but in **Philippines 4:13** Paul tells us that:

I can do all things through Christ who strengthens me.

How amazing is that!

It's incredible, it is wonderful, it is glorious! We must rejoice!

Let us take a look at **Psalm 127: 3-5 Behold, children are a heritage from the Lord, the fruit of the womb is a reward. Like arrows in the hand of a warrior; so are the children of one's youth. Happy is the man who has his quiver full of them; they shall not be ashamed, but shall speak with their enemies in the gate.**

We need to, and must, honour our children; they are gifts from God.

1John 3:7-8 Little children, let no one deceive you. He who practices righteousness is righteous, just as He is righteous.

We don't need to be theologians to comprehend the word of God; we only need the Holy Spirit who will lead us into discernment and all truth.

We must always be aware however, that the devil prowls round constantly. **1Peter 5:8 Be sober, be vigilant, because your adversary the devil, as a roaring lion, walks about seeking whom he may devour.**

2Corinthians 11:14 ….For Satan himself transforms himself into an angel of light. He is nothing but a liar and a deceiver and we need to be aware of this.

There are many, many parents who are unable to have children and this is surely a sadness for them to bear. However, their barrenness does not mean that God does not bless them. His blessings are treasures and many, and though he may withhold child birth from some, He has a purpose.

Isaiah 54:1 "Sing, O barren, you who have not borne! Break forth into singing, and cry aloud. You have not travailed with child! For more are the children of the desolate than the children of the married woman." says the Lord.

God does not think as we do, nor does He follow the paths we take. It is good to remind ourselves of this when we struggle with matters that are beyond us.

Isaiah 55:8-9 For my thoughts are not your thoughts. Nor are your ways My ways, says the Lord, For as the heavens are higher than the earth, so are My ways higher than your ways. And My thoughts than your thoughts.

In **2 Samuel 6:23** we read that Michal, the daughter of Saul, did not have a child. **Therefore Michal the daughter of Saul had no children to the day of her death.** But sadly it was a punishment. It would be worthwhile to read the chapter so as to learn the reason why God inflicted punishment.

In **Luke 23:28-29.** Jesus considers it a blessing not to have children, especially in the 'last days'. **"Daughters of Jerusalem, do not weep for Me, but weep for yourselves and for your children. For indeed the days are coming in which they will say, 'Blessed are the barren, wombs that never bore, and breasts which never nursed.'"**

However, there are women in Scripture who were barren, but conceived in their later years. We'll start of with Sarah, Abraham's wife.

Abraham was told by an angel sent from God, that Sarah will conceive, and Sarah was listening in the wings, so when she heard this, it made her laugh! **Genesis 18:11-14 Now Sarah and Abraham were old, well advanced in age, and Sarah had passed the age of childbearing. Therefore Sarah laughed within herself, saying 'After I have grown old, shall I have pleasure, my lord being old also?' And the Lord said to Abraham. 'Why did Sarah laugh, saying, 'Shall I surely bare a child, since I am old?'**

Now, **verse 14** is the crunch. **"Is anything too hard for the Lord? At the appointed time I will return to you, according to the time of life and Sarah shall have a son."** (underlining mine) Suggest to read the proceeding verses so as to fully appreciate the situation.

What a promise! And know, as Christians, we must know, and believe that - nothing, nothing, absolutely nothing, nothing is too difficult for the Lord. We can find this in **Jeremiah 32:17** from which Don Moen, an American Christian singer and song writer, produced a song.

There was also Hannah in **1 Samuel 1:1-5,** Rebecca in **Genesis 25:21, Rachel in Genesis 30:22-24**, and in **Judges 30:22-24** there is Manoah's wife, who is nameless, and married to Samson; Elizabeth married to John, who we know as John the Baptist. **Luke 1:6-17.** Poor John, he didn't believe the angel! **18-23** and then we read in **24-25** a miracle! All make interesting reading.

We have a wonderful God and in recognising this, we should automatically turn our faces away from the distractions of the world, those unnecessary things that really don't do anything for our spiritual lives. Children are astute, in that, though they are not always able to verbalise their thoughts and feelings, recognise those things that are not right. There was a child who, though believed in God, did not know Jesus, but every time she heard his name used as a swear word, she would recoil. Her spirit recognised that this was wrong.

The children of this generation have no option but to grow up in a digital world. It is thrown at them at birth. They appear to be constantly involved with their mobile phones, ipads, ipods and iphones, (notice the 'i') face book, message, selfies and numerous unsuitable apps. Concern is, the harm they are doing not only to our children but adults as well. 'What must we do Lord to save our little ones?' should be our cry, but the majority are deaf and blind to the deception that is taking place under our very eyes, and there needs to be an awakening. How?

By prayer and praise.

(The undermentioned is an extract from the writer's last book "My Kingdom is Not of This World.")

(Because this present book is written with regard to not stopping our children coming to the Lord, the author feels it is important to refresh our memories, always bearing in mind that we will be made accountable for our actions, but knowing that there is **There is no condemnation to those in Christ Jesus, who do not walk according to the flesh, but according to the Spirit. Romans 8:1**)

Sadly, some churches today are calling people to church by installing a golf course, a helter skelter so as visitors can have a better view of the ceiling; a bouncy castle, coffee, tea and biscuits and book stalls. Well, what's wrong with that, you might ask.

Let us take a look at **Matthew's Gospel 21:12-13. Then Jesus went into the temple of God and drove out all those who bought and sold in the temple, and overturned the tables of the those who sold doves. And He said to them,! "It is written,**

'My house shall be called a <u>house of prayer</u>, but you have made it a den of thieves.'" (underlining mine)

The disrespect now prominent in some church buildings and cathedrals is very much evident. This is not standing in judgement, it is simply stating an observation and fact that <u>the world has come into the buildings abiding within its people</u>. Mobile phones are used for hymns and recording services; people text and receive texts during services. Can we really not function without phones for an hour or so? Let us not forget <u>Who</u> God is. We must always remember that we have a Holy God, and He will not be mocked.

In **Matthew 26:38-40** when Jesus and His disciples went into the garden of Gethsemane and He asked them to wait for Him whilst He went and prayed. What did they do? - they slept.

He went a little further and fell on His face, and prayed, saying, "O My Father, if it is possible, let this cup pass from Me; nevertheless, not as I will, but as You will." Then He came to the disciples and found them sleeping and said to Peter.

"What! <u>Could you not watch with Me</u> <u>one hour</u>? (Perhaps today He would say 'Are you still on your phones?') (underlining mine) **Watch and pray lest you enter into temptation. The spirit is indeed willing, but the flesh is weak."**

Church goers give their time in attending services and whilst there so many hold on to their mobiles, send texts, read texts, so not fully entering, if at all, to the praise and worship due to their God. What an insult!

Man may change as he 'progresses', but **Jesus Christ is the same yesterday, today and forever. Hebrews 13:8** and He will not be mocked, as previously stated, which we can read in **Galatians 6:7 Do not be deceived, God is not mocked; for whatever a man sows, that he will reap.**

There is a laissez faire attitude. We are not setting the right example to our little ones.

The church building or a place that represents it, isn't a playground – it is a sacred and holy place where God's people are able to set themselves apart from the world for a while. They were built to glorify God, not the things of the world. Children are easily influenced and if they see that the building is treated like a play area, they naturally follow suit.

God is not a spoil sport – far from it. He wants us to enjoy the fun things of this world – golf, slides, bouncy castles, coffee mornings and book sales – but there are other places for these. Would we expect to find the above in a library, or in a head master/mistress's office, or 10 Downing Street? No. First of all there wouldn't be space. But for small tea parties and book stalls there would be – but would they take place? No again. These rooms are set aside for the function they were built for, and thus respected for these.

The church was once a Holy Place, a Temple just for God,
Then worldly men began their games, seems they couldn't give a jot.
With stalls set up to buy and sell, the place is desecrated,
Teas and coffees, cakes and more, a sanctuary not sacred.
There are not so blind that cannot see these things that have been done,
believing them to be worthwhile, for God wants us to have fun.
Oh yes, He does, that is so true, for He gave us smiles and laughter,
But let's treat His House with due respect,
and keep worldly things for after.
We must teach His love to every child, when we sit and stand and walk,
teach them to pray and praise the Lord and speak no idle talk;
To give honour to His House of praise, and listen quietly,
No added music to His word, no need for its company.

The following is an example how many in the world live their lives, and, it was written long before the internet entered into the public domain.

TALK TO THE HAND THE FACE AIN'T LISTENING

Have you noticed in the last few years that a lot of folk do not listen any more? - it seems others are a bore.

There is no interest in a two-way conversation, they either blabber on incessantly about the 'I' or just stare on some pretext or another; or are they simply shy?

If one dares to give some information of ones self, not indeed to hold complete attention, but to simply mention this or that, inducing friendly chat, their eyes glaze over, ears close up, and before one knows it, they have shut you up.

I do not put all humans in this selfish category but must insist on this observation – that many folk now desist in making conversation.

"Talk to the hand, the face ain't listening"; I was aghast but admit I laughed upon first hearing this expression – but soon I heard an annotation of their views – we're not listening to you, and don't want to.

What has happened to the peoples of today – is this world wide this attitude that is so very rude and such a shame – I wonder who's to blame?

In this particular society materialism has brought about the violation of the laws that govern.

Discipline has disappeared and children now are reared by parents doing as they are told.

The plot's been lost and at such a cost, it's quite incredible.

The television leaves its mark, its mark indelible upon, not just the young, but older folk as well.

It seems they're bound up in a hell, a whirlpool of deceit, worldly offers lifting them too high off their feet, so high they cannot see for looking at what's cooking down below.

Holding doors allowing one to enter through is something of the past.

No please, thank you, yes or no, just grunts that leave one feeling somewhat harsh toward those who have their hands before their faces.

They embrace a different world, a world within this world, with a gulf which now separates mankind from himself – not hearing, seeing, introspective, not reflective, can't be, for they cannot hear or see, just want to be without a face, leaving a trace of debris as they journey on, lost it seems forever.

Surely with endeavour they can be found again – if only they would lighten up, turn off the noise, unplug the ears and listen to the silence in their souls – there is time for them to be made whole.

Looking at **Deuteronomy 6:5-7** we read: **You shall love the Lord your God with all your heart, with all your soul, and**

with all your strength. And these words which I command you today shall be in your heart. You shall teach them diligently to your children and shall talk of them when you sit in your house, when you walk by the way, and you lie down, and when you rise up.

And as we pray for our children, let us take heed to what **James** says in **Chapter 5:16 …..The effective, fervent prayer of a righteous man avails much.**

Having a position of authority quite often gives one an air of self-righteousness, and though Jesus spoke as one in authority, in doing so He was humble and righteous.

How do Christians avoid becoming 'know alls'? We always need to be teachable. We need to humbly acknowledge the truth that we are never above learning. We must avoid having an idealistic attitude and be tolerant of our own failings and the failings we perceive in others, allowing God to deal with us all gently, but firmly.

There was a gentleman who was blessed with a gift for working with the young. He used to run a youth group, organizing various outings, coupling them with bargains. The group meetings took place on Friday and Saturday nights, with around 50-70 youngsters in attendance. There was football and table tennis, and an area where the children were able to run around, using up their energies running and skipping and playing 'catch'. A food bar with soft drinks was available and rooms in which they could chat. There was also a huge video screen, on which videos for mixed ages were shown.

Some parents felt the latter was unnecessary, particularly as they considered some of the films unsuitable. However, this man insisted that they were what the <u>children wanted</u>. Was this attitude wise? It was argued that more family orientated films would be more appropriate, thereby allowing the children to absorb a finer quality of viewing. Sadly, he was not in agreement.

God lays down the moral code for our children's upbringing, so we must be answerable for carrying it through.

<u>We must not stop the little children coming to Him</u>. Babies and young children are often put in front of the television to keep them occupied. A modern nanny. Harmless? What has happened to the play pen? To allow these little angels to be kept occupied by placing them constantly in front of the television whilst the parent is busy, is not healthy. The play pen is a far better helper with toys for amusement.

'Mums to be' have a tremendous influence on their unborn babies, surely influence does not stop at birth. There are many Christian parents who read Scripture to their unborn babies, sing songs and tell them they are loved. Scientific research has shown that the unborn baby reacts to a mother's emotional and physical experiences. Does the response stop at birth? Of course not! What a mother eats determines, not only her health, but the health, growth and weight of her baby during and after pregnancy. Smoking and drinking have detrimental effects on both. We cannot ignore the fact that a parent's influence formulate the mind, body and spirit of their offspring. Don't we hang on to a lot of what our parents taught us, whether good or bad?

Children have been, and are still being robbed of their right to be innocent, something which was once considered to be so precious.

(It still is so very precious.) How many children are untainted today from watching corrupt television, logging onto the internet, face book and the different apps. on their smart phones? These appliances maybe here to stay, but we really need to think seriously about the way we use them. Yes, we may make excuses for various reasons, but does God go along with our worldly excuses?

Jesus tells us in **Matthew 5:13-16** that: **You are the salt of the earth, but if the salt loses its flavour how shall it be seasoned? It is then good for nothing but to be thrown out and trampled under foot by men. You are the light of the world. A city that is set on a hill cannot be hidden. Nor do they light a lamp and put it under a basket, but on a lamp stand and it gives light to all the house. Let your light so shine before men, that they may see your good works and glorify your Father in Heaven.**

Let us awake O Christian to our rightful duty and bring up our sons and daughters in the love and fear of the Lord. If children continually have their heads down pressing buttons, how are they to see the beauty in the world that God created?

The following celebrates His magnificent artistry.

> *Lord, you took your paint box out*
> *the other day, I know.*
> *I see the colours in the trees,*
> *There's a sparkle and a glow.*
> *Your colours are so very rich,*
> *so deep, so beautiful;*

*The very essence of Your love
is plain in such a skill.*

*The falling leaves, they way goodbye,
Another season ended.
Your paint brush moves across the sky,
Your graciousness all blended.
A flock of birds in silent form
You dab upon the blue;
a ray of light upon the green,
a wonderment of you.*

*No human artist can describe
in paint on canvas board,
the falling leaves, the gentle breeze,*

Your creation Lord.
With paint and skill and gifted mind
he can create a picture;
but not like yours, for Yours is real,
and countless times far richer.

There are words of tremendous encouragement in Scripture, and we certainly need to encourage one another more and more in these difficult days, and not become despondent. We need to feel God's concern and assert to His convictions, which would enable Him to see our love, great regard and respect for His Holiness.

We mustn't afford ourselves to become disgruntled, and think that God is a misery. He is far from it. He has blessed the human race with a gift of humour and fun, which are also part of His nature. He has a pure mind, and therefore we must strive for purity in our life style, making sure we are doing our best to be on line with Him.

It is healthy and necessary for us to take time to 'smell the roses', that is, to relax, get life into proper perspective, rejoice in and enjoy His creation.

TAKE TIME TO SMELL THE ROSES

Life imposes so much stress
that it's best to take time to
smell the roses.
Be sure this metaphor is to
implore one to do other
things apart from
daily work.
It is so important not to shirk
at having play time.
Adults must be children too,
not take the view that play is
not for them.
The mind and body work as one and having fun destroys the toxins in
the blood, endorphins laugh as stress is cut – at least by half.
To take time out when one is used to being very busy,
is not at first so easy, but with effort and endurance,
eventually one sees it's like a health insurance.
One laughs and smiles more often, feels a sense of peace,
and then, before one knows it, has settled in the niche of -
taking time to smell the roses.

Romans 12:2 And do not be conformed to this world, but be transformed by the renewing of your mind, so that you prove

what the will of God is, that which is good and acceptable and perfect.

In other words, though in this world, we must not be of it. We need to have the courage of our convictions, which is our belief in a Holy God, refusing to be fed by the world. When the Pharisees asked Jesus if it was lawful to pay taxes to Caesar, Jesus asked for a coin, and asked the question.

Whose head in this, whose inscription? And they answered, "Caesar's". His reply – **"Render therefore to Caesar things that are Caesar's and to God the things that are God's." Matthew 2:20.**

We must do just that - leave the things of the world to those who want them and take the holy things of God and give them to Him – bless Him, honour Him and glorify Him. It is so easy to compromise – why do we?

It is essential to always remember that children believe in the magic of life. Not conjurers and funny clowns, (though these are part of childhood) just simple innocence, until such time they burst out of their cocoons of safety and are ready to take on the world, hopefully having been brought up in the love and knowledge of Jesus. Yes, some go astray, some don't, but no matter, He loves every child and will never leave or forsakes any, and there would always be a welcome forgiveness at the end of the day.

(There is an awe-inspiring book called 'The Return of the Prodigal Son' by Henri J.M. Nouwen (1932-1996) in which he describes his study of a painting of the same by Rembrandt, the Dutch artist of the 17th century. His insight into the artist's portrayal of forgiveness is quite unique, and well worth reading.)

We, too, like the Prodigal's father, no doubt wait with bated breath for the return of some of our children, welcoming them with open arms and a forgiving heart.

How do we encourage our children to be 'in' the world and not 'of' it?

If we teach them from a young age about Jesus, it makes life much simpler as they grow up with wanting to please Him, how much He loves them, and learning that there are many things in the world that <u>appear</u> harmless, but are not pleasing to God. We can always give examples, one being why must we not watch certain television programmes? There are of course plenty others which children will understand. We have to be set apart from the uncleanliness of the world, though, it really has to go without saying, not in a 'we are better than thou' attitude, but in obedience and love for the Lord – as we are commanded and should want to do. (Christians are better off, not better than.)

What does the world about us have to offer children in their every day lives outside of their homes?

There are many healthy activities for them to pursue and take part in, where they can gain confidence by forming friendships with new children, teaching them about sharing with, and caring for others.

Unfortunately, or rather, regretfully and sadly, today many children are constantly on their phones, tangled up in the world's empty offerings, thus missing out on their childhood bestowed upon them by God. They have no alternative but to grow up in a digital world, but it is not beyond control. Even so, alas, they are encouraged by friends and parents who are forever on their phones to do the same. Adults are example setters. We need to seriously pray about our attitude toward the world and our Holy God with His expectations, and of course our own. We must honour Him through honouring our children, who in turn will learn the meaning of honour.

John 12:26 If anyone serves me, let him follow Me; and where I am, there My servant will be also. If anyone serves Me, him My Father will honour.

Though children are born into the world 'bathed in innocence, no sin', as is written in the last line of the poem at the beginning of the book, we do know that they are tainted with Adam's sin – the sin of disobedience, known generally as 'original sin'. This, as we are also aware, has plagued mankind since that unhappy day in the Garden of Eden.

Looking at the world, it appears that Lucifer, the devil, has won, but we know that Jesus ultimately has the victory, achieved by the Cross. So harbouring this knowledge, we must continually look toward His Cross with gratitude, and teach our children to do the same – not in a melodramatic way, but with sadness, and then joy at His Resurrection.

The Holy Spirit is truly sensitive to youngsters, knowing and understanding them, giving them that childlike perception that they need. It is quite wonderful to watch children skipping in delight at life, and playing innocently. Of course there are times where the sin of disobedience is prevalent, but as parents, teachers and friends it is worthwhile to allow and welcome these times to speak to us, so as we can examine our own activities that are not pleasing to God. Children can be masters at teaching.

It is vital to keep our lives in the right perspective as we live in this world and not of it. We are not expected to live as monks or nuns or in desert caves, therefore becoming totally separate! That would be ridiculous. God accredited us with common sense, and from a young age we know the difference between right and wrong, good and bad. We have choices and children must be taught this. Prayer with them is so important as well, probably making the time for it short, so as they don't shrug their shoulders with boredom, and allowing them to express themselves in their own way.

Doubtlessly we have to show honest and worthwhile leadership in bringing up our children as Christians, but there is no need for us to panic or be anxious, for **'if God is for us who can be against us?' Romans 8:31.** and **Phillipians 4:13 I can do all things through Christ who strengthens me.**

We also need to wear his armour – **Ephesians 6:11-18.**

These scriptures are food, the spiritual food of which we need doses and doses, holding on to what Jesus tells us in Matthew 4:4.

"….Man shall not live by bread alone, but by every word coming out of the mouth of God."

One of the first words we say to a little child when he/she has become aware, is 'no'. But they always want their own way, and unless we are strict but fair from the very start, the youngsters will be confused. Rebelliousness begins early and we know that babies are cute, beautiful and delicate, but very knowing!

They thrive on discipline, and really embrace it, as even as adults we should. A disciplined child is so lovely to see – unspoilt, gracious and pleasing. He or she may not always be obedient, but overall is a pleasant child. No one is faultless – we were all born into sin, and though repentant, we are still aware of its presence and temptations. Let us not allow ourselves to have the attitude of Oscar Wilde in his book The Picture of Dorian Gray 'The only way to get rid of temptation is to yield to it...'. As a joke, it is amusing! But when we are serious as when contemplating God's Word, let us go beyond those thoughts.

Children are up against a great deal of evil, much of it springing from the internet. It cannot be emphasised enough that we need to be sagacious as to its use, as we, too, are inclined to be taken in by much of what it has to offer. What chance do children have if we as Christians are forever seeking our pleasures on the www – world wide web, which in Hebrew and Greek is the number 666. If we take a look at the book of **Revelation Chapter 13** we can read about this www. Mankind is manipulated by the father of lies and is easily hoodwinked, so it is necessary to give children a healthy life style, helping them and ourselves by distracting us all from the constancy of the internet,

Lamentably, it is only the older generation that can recall life as it was before the nation, and the world as a whole, were plunged so deeply into modern technology. Regretfully, because of the generation gap, those that have grown wise with age, are considered by many as fuddy-duddies, without any perception of the modern way of life. But older people know that 'old heads cannot be put on young shoulders'.

There are a number of proverbs which are worth reading with regard to wisdom and age.

Isaiah 46.4 Even to your old age, I am He, and even to gray hairs I will carry you! I have made, and I will bear; even I will carry you, and will deliver you.

Psalm 91 With long life I will satisfy him, and show him my salvation.

2 Corinthians 4-16 Therefore we do not lose heart. Even though our outward man is perishing, yet the inward man is being renewed day by day.

Old age needs to be respected in that the elderly have experienced life and all its hand-outs, and like every generation before, has, and still has to, deal with new and different inventions, thus altering their ways of living, be it for good or bad. Christians need more and more wisdom given from the Holy Spirit, to discern between righteousness and integrity and corruption and wickedness. It is a never ending battle, but if we remember to reflect on **2 Chronicles 20 'the battle belongs to the Lord.'** there is no need to become stressed and weary; we just need to put our concerns into His wonderful hands, believing that He has everything under control, and in trusting Him we will know what to do. He permits and forbids as He sees fit. There are many verses in the Bible where we can read about being given permission or otherwise.

Let us return to the beginning where we read **Matthew's Gospel Chapter 19:13** when the disciples rebuked the little children and Jesus says **"Let the little children come to Me and do not <u>forbid</u> them, for of such is the Kingdom of Heaven.**

Now verse 14 **But when Jesus saw it, he was greatly displeased and said to them. "<u>Let (permit</u>) the little children to come to me, and do not <u>forbid</u> them, for of such is the kingdom of God. Assuredly, I say to you, <u>whoever does not receive the kingdom of God as a little child will by no means enter it</u>." And he took them up in his arms, put his hands on them and blessed them.** (underlining mine)

So, too, today, let us not stop the little children from being blessed by our Lord because of our self-indulgences and ignorance.

We believe as born again Christians that we are going to be welcomed into the Kingdom of God. **Matthew 7:21-23** but let us not be casual. When we are all gathered before Him, and He divides us into those who will be with Him and those who will not, stating all the things that we did or did not do, will we be innocent or guilty of not allowing our children to be fed unsuitable information, happenings and junk on the internet? We need to 'search out our hearts' in humility.

Proverbs 20:9 Who can say, "I have made my heart clean, I am pure from sin"?

And in **Proverbs 20:7 The righteous man walks in his integrity; His children are blessed after him.**

Children need, at the start of their lives, to be wrapped up in 'cotton wool', respected and loved. The love and respect is to continue throughout their lives, but the cotton wool must be gradually removed as they enter more fully into the fallen world. Children's books can be a wonderful blessing for their learning and grasping an understanding of life. There are many Christian, Christian based and even non Christian stories that make healthy and easy reading. Alas, there have always been children who do not enjoy the written word, but sadly more so today, having preference for their smart phones. Consequently they deny themselves the full use of their imaginations, are not able to interact so well with others, they miss out on fun stories, which would help in giving them conversation and they have minimal vocabulary and poor spelling.

One might argue that books and language are obtainable, like most things, on the internet. Perhaps so, but what is it doing to a child's mind as he/she is forever clicking from one thing to another? They need to look up and be aware. They need to interact personally with adults and friends.

Advertisements on Christian television encourage children to use apps, to read, watch films and play games on their smart phones. Is it all right to ask, 'Where is the discernment in this?' It might be okay for a very short span of time, but to be on a regular and daily basis must be detrimental to their lives. Having a book in the hand allows children to concentrate on just that – the book, and playing games with others is so much fun, natural and freeing.

The subject of mental health is at the top of the agenda for discussion these days more than it ever was before social media and all it involves, came on the scene. It is a strange happening that our youngsters and parents are so distraught, one wonders if they are deprived of ordinary common sense.

Satan is having a field day with everyone so caught up with the internet, he has blinded most by his evil tactics, removing all sound judgement. We have become a despairing people, yet at the same time maintaining that we are content and fulfilled.

Trickery is rampant, but if we walk hand in hand with our Lord, we do not have to be deluded, just as Christ wasn't when he was in the desert, hungry and vulnerable. **Matthew 4:1-11.** But His eyes were on His Father, as ours must be.

We stop the little children coming to Jesus by constantly living in the world, partaking of all that is futile and wrong, being part of its deceit. We need to remember that Jesus says that He is the Way, the Truth and the Life and on admitting and following this, we are set free. We need to examine our hearts, being totally honest with our inner selves, and if we find that we are over the border into the world's offerings, repent, and we will be given the strength and the ability to back out or change direction.

We must be round the clock aware of being deceived into supposing that all the offerings we encounter on the internet are okay. The fox deceived Red Riding Hood by his disguises, and as Jesus called Herod a fox in **Luke's gospel 13:32** that is exactly what the devil is in all of his disguises – a fox. This sly animal is also known to be unclean - as is Satan.

In the world of so called 'sweet offerings' with all the 'must haves', but are 'all right' 'must haves', deception is at its peak. Children are defenceless, and with the shallowness and unawareness of many unwise Christian adults, they are left bereft, not knowing of God's love for them. However, unwise Christian adults can receive wisdom by just asking for it as **James** says in his epistle **Chapter 1:5.** We have no excuse for lacking wisdom, for if we believe in the Holy Spirit, we know that He is always at hand to guide us in righteousness.

Having been asked by Jesus Himself not to stop the little children coming to Him should encourage us to separate ourselves from the world, always being aware that we are fully accountable for their spiritual well being until such time they become independent. We are to be 100% with our Lord. It is necessary to examine and to be totally honest with ourselves, secure in the knowledge that the Lord loves us and sees into the depths of our hearts and our thoughts, knowing our desires, and all that bothers us, and so much more. Jesus is there to heal and to forgive and respects those who respect Him. Our admission and turning away from things that are wrong sets us free, allowing us to embrace self respect and a mighty respect for our Holy God.

Psalm 139 makes for a beautiful read – and the last two **verses 23-24** - a prayer. Search me, **O God, and know my heart; try me, and know my anxieties; And see if there is any wicked way in me, and lead me in the way everlasting.**

Train up a child in the way he should go, and when he is old he will not depart from it. Proverbs 22:4.

www.ingramcontent.com/pod-product-compliance
Lightning Source LLC
Chambersburg PA
CBHW071549080526
44588CB00011B/1836